I0078899

Six Contemporary Piano Pieces

by Margaret Brandman

Exclusive Distributors for Australia and New Zealand
Encore Music Distributors 227 Napier St. Fitzroy. 3065 Victoria Australia
Ph +61 3 9415 6677 Facsimile 61 3 9415 6655
Email sales@encoremusic.com.au

This book © Copyright 2020 by Margaret Brandman trading as Jazzem Music
46 Gerrale St, Cronulla NSW 2230 Australia

ISBN 978-0-949683-46-5
ISMN 979-0-720010-01-4
ORDER NUMBER MMP 8057

International Copyright Secured (APRA/AMCOS) All Rights Reserved
www.margaretbrandman.com

Unauthorised reproduction of any part of this publication by any means including
photocopying is an infringement of copyright.

For more information on Margaret Brandman's collection of compositions, recordings and DVDs, please visit:

www.margaretbrandman.com

Contents

* — Also suitable for classical Accordion

Six Contemporary Pieces

Piano performance pieces with a hint of Jazz

Intermediate to Advanced level

Title	Grade

Badinarie No. 1

5

This work is composed using the Balinese pelog scale and incorporates changing time signatures. The pensive introduction is followed by more animated section with flowing 16th note passages exploring the possibilities inherent in the Balinese scale and touching on the C minor tonality for variety.

Badinarie No.2

5

A rhapsodic work based on the tonal centre of E with the use of Aeolian, Dorian modal melodies and extended harmonies. The work begins in a free flowing style incorporating changing metres for the first six measures, and then continues in Simple Quadruple time till the end.

Invention

6

Classical Invention form with a modern twist, based on a theme comprising of Rising 5th or Falling 4th intervals which lends a very contemporary sound to the piece. This piece uses contrapuntal devices for two- part writing. These include: Subject, Answer, Episode, Thematic inversion, Rhythmic Augmentation and Rhythmic Diminution. The 5/4 and 5/8 time signatures add spice and interest to the work.

Tango Tranquille

7

The 'Tempo rubato' introduction is richly textured using chromatic harmonies leading to the tonic Cadd^9 chord in measure seven. A second episode leads to the main theme beginning in measure 18. Here the tango rhythm is introduced and, the melody continues to incorporate the 32nd note motif from the opening measure. The middle section of the work is of contrasting style, beginning in E minor and making use of some hand-over-hand techniques. The final uplifting, spirited section is a variation of the main tango theme in the key of Db – a semitone higher than the original statement of the theme.

Sunshowers on the River

5

This work is in Theme and Variations form. The opening theme is composed using the pentatonic scale on E which lends a bright sound to the melody. The time signature is 7/4. This piece includes an improvisatory section in free time, which can be extended by the performer at their leisure, prior to the final vigorous statement of the theme at a distance of two octaves between the hands ending on the sunny and bright sounding E Major 9$^{(13)}$ chord.

Mini-Suite

5

This work displays multiple instances of thematic manipulation using both baroque polyphonic writing techniques and contemporary techniques as used in serial composition. The final section is more chordal and syncopated lending some Jazz elements to the work. Although this piece begins on the tonal centre of Eb, it concludes a fifth lower, on Ab.

Badinarie No. 1

Margaret S. Brandman

© Copyright 2020 Margaret Brandman Trading as Jazzem Music.
International copyright secured. APRA/AMCOS. All rights reserved.
Photocopying is illegal.

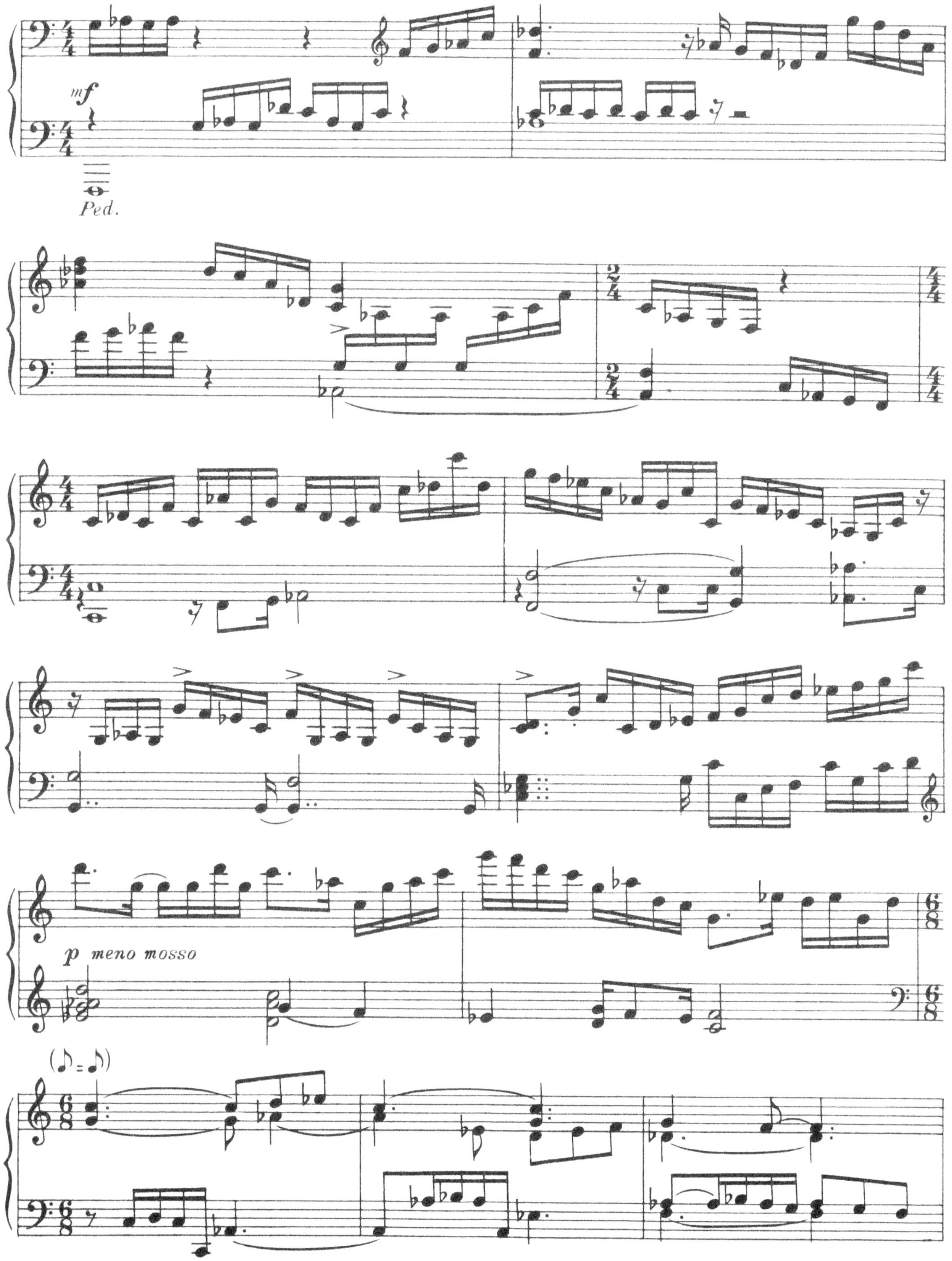
mf
Ped.
p meno mosso

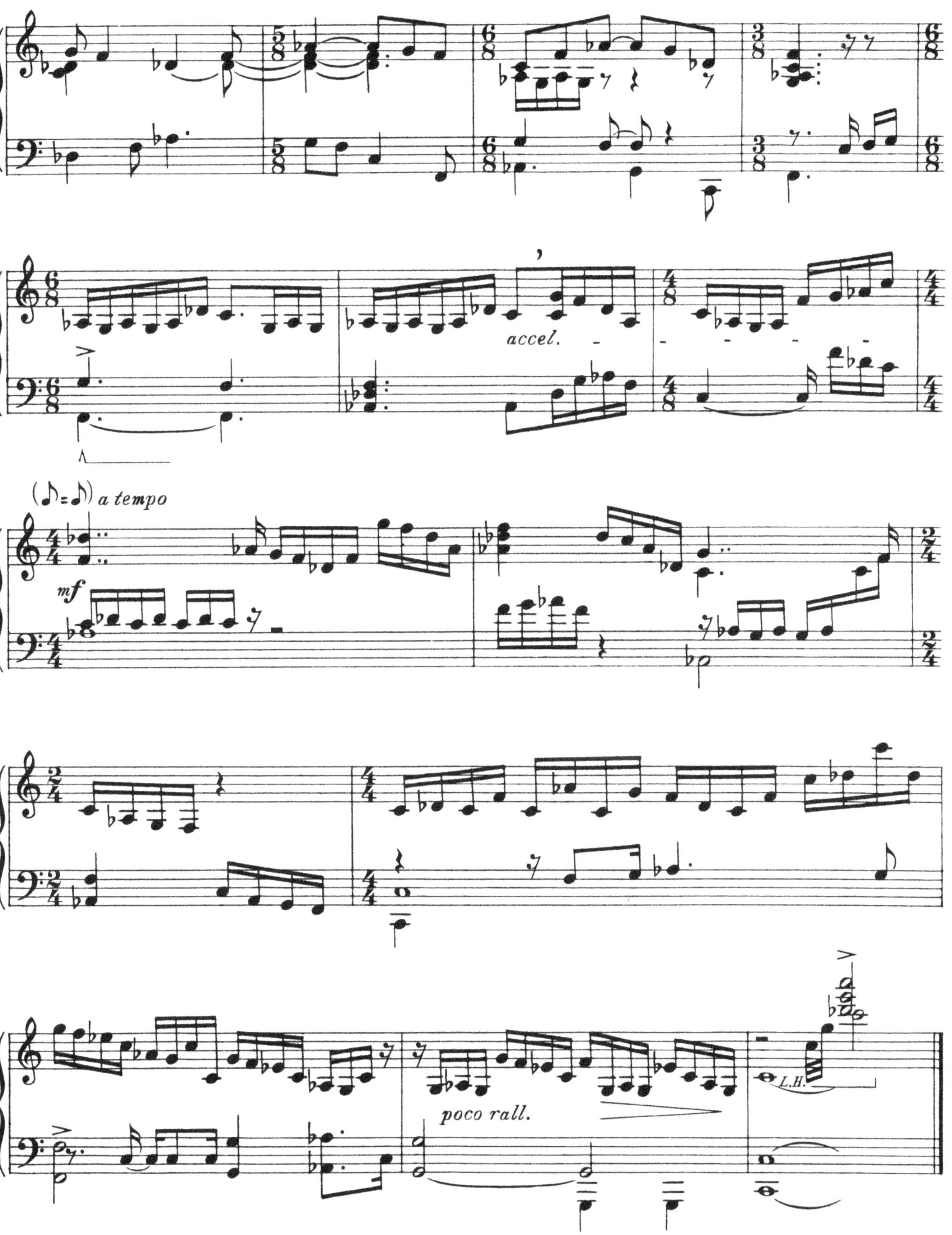
accel.
(♪=♪) a tempo
mf
poco rall.
L.H.

Badinarie No. 2

Margaret S. Brandman

Allegretto (*In a flowing style*)

© Copyright 2020 Margaret Brandman Trading as Jazzem Music.
International copyright secured. APRA/AMCOS. All rights reserved.
Photocopying is illegal.

D. 𝄋 al Coda

poco rall.

⊕ CODA

Invention

Margaret S. Brandman

Allegretto ♩ = 70

Ped. *lightly throughout*

© Copyright 2020 Margaret Brandman Trading as Jazzem Music.
International copyright secured. APRA/AMCOS. All rights reserved.
Photocopying is illegal.

cresc. - - poco - a - poco
mf
rall.
mf a tempo accel.
a tempo
Allargando
mf

Tango Tranquille

Margaret S. Brandman

© Copyright 2020 Margaret Brandman Trading as Jazzem Music.
International copyright secured. APRA/AMCOS. All rights reserved.
Photocopying is illegal.

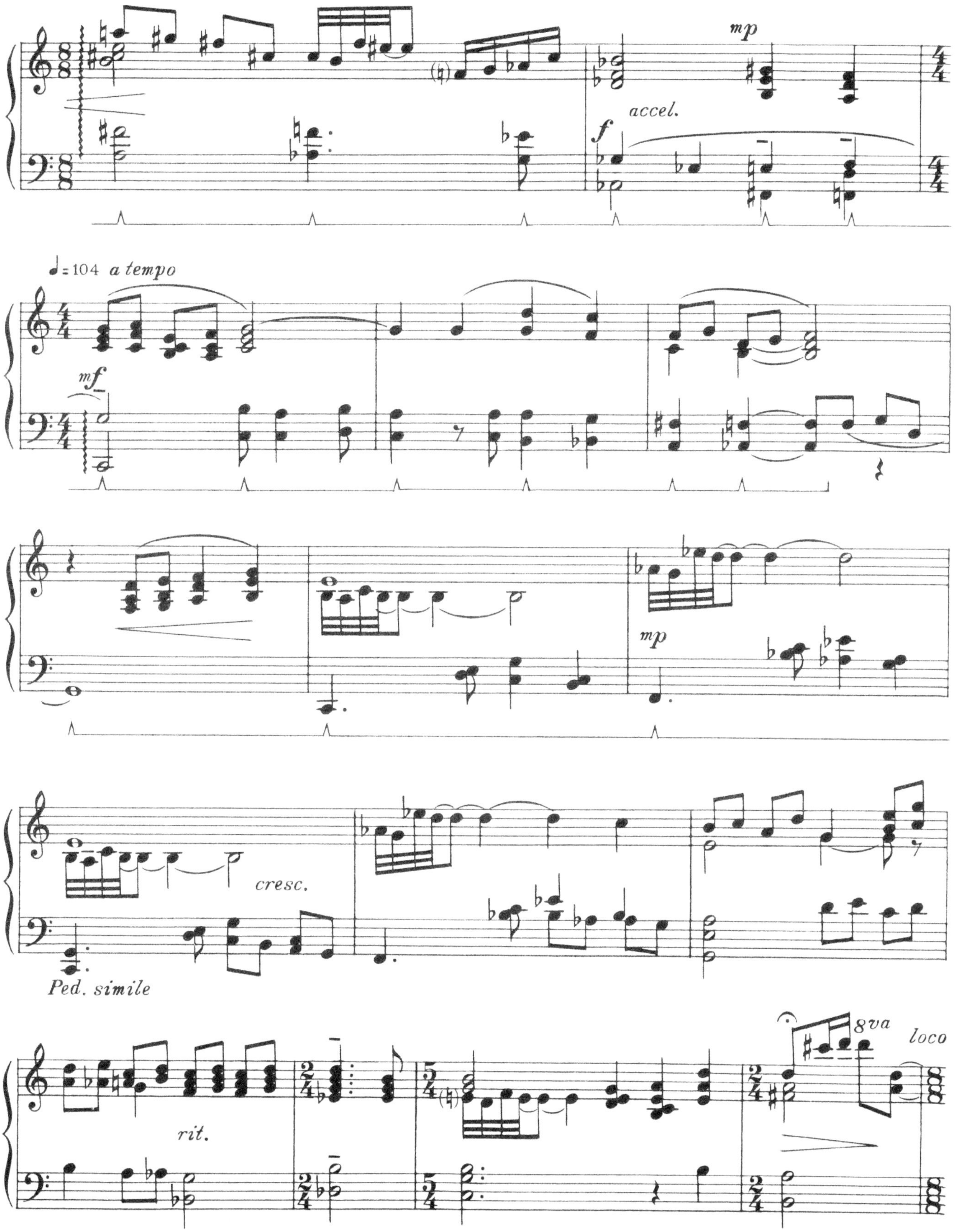
mp
accel.
f
♩=104 a tempo
mf
mp
cresc.
Ped. simile
rit.
8va
loco

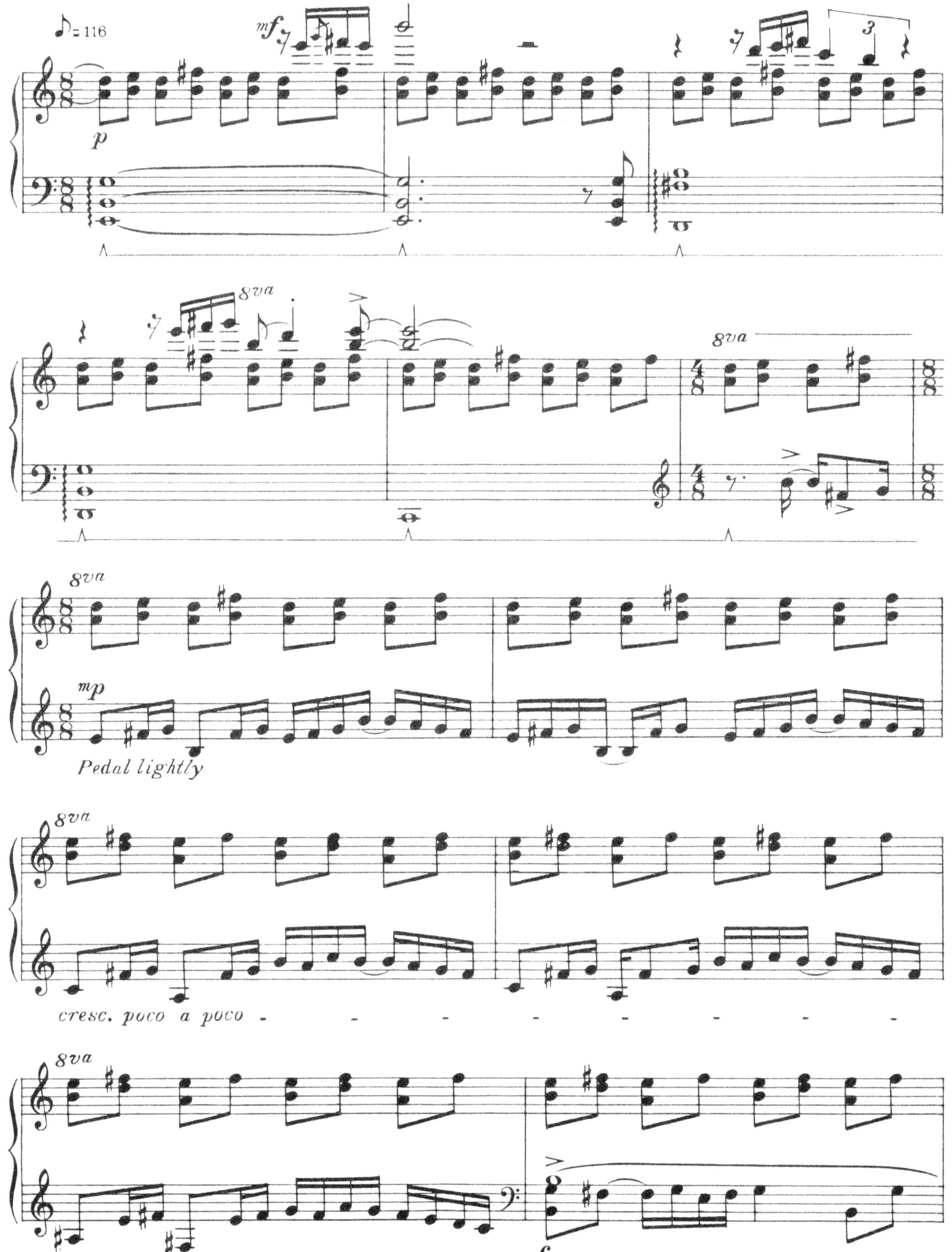
♪= 116
mf
p
3
8va
8va
mp
Pedal lightly
8va
cresc. poco a poco
8va
f

8va
loco
8va
rit.
ff
a tempo
mf hold back
♩= 84
♩= 100 With spirit
f
Ped simile
8va
rit.
8va

Sunshowers On the River
(Variations in a Modern Style)

Margaret S. Brandman

© Copyright 2020 Margaret Brandman Trading as Jazzem Music.
International copyright secured. APRA/AMCOS. All rights reserved.
Photocopying is illegal.

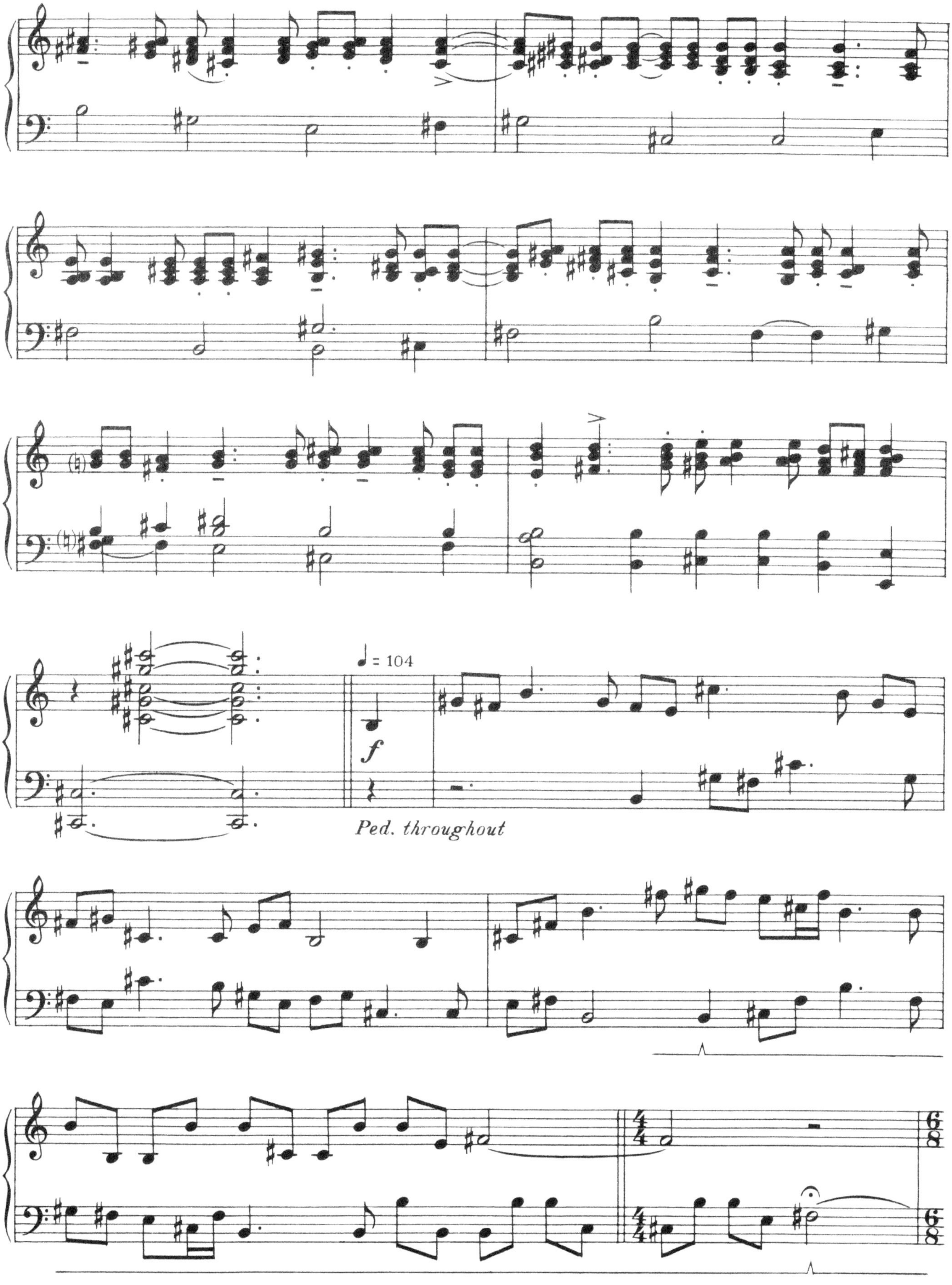
♩ = 104
f
Ped. throughout

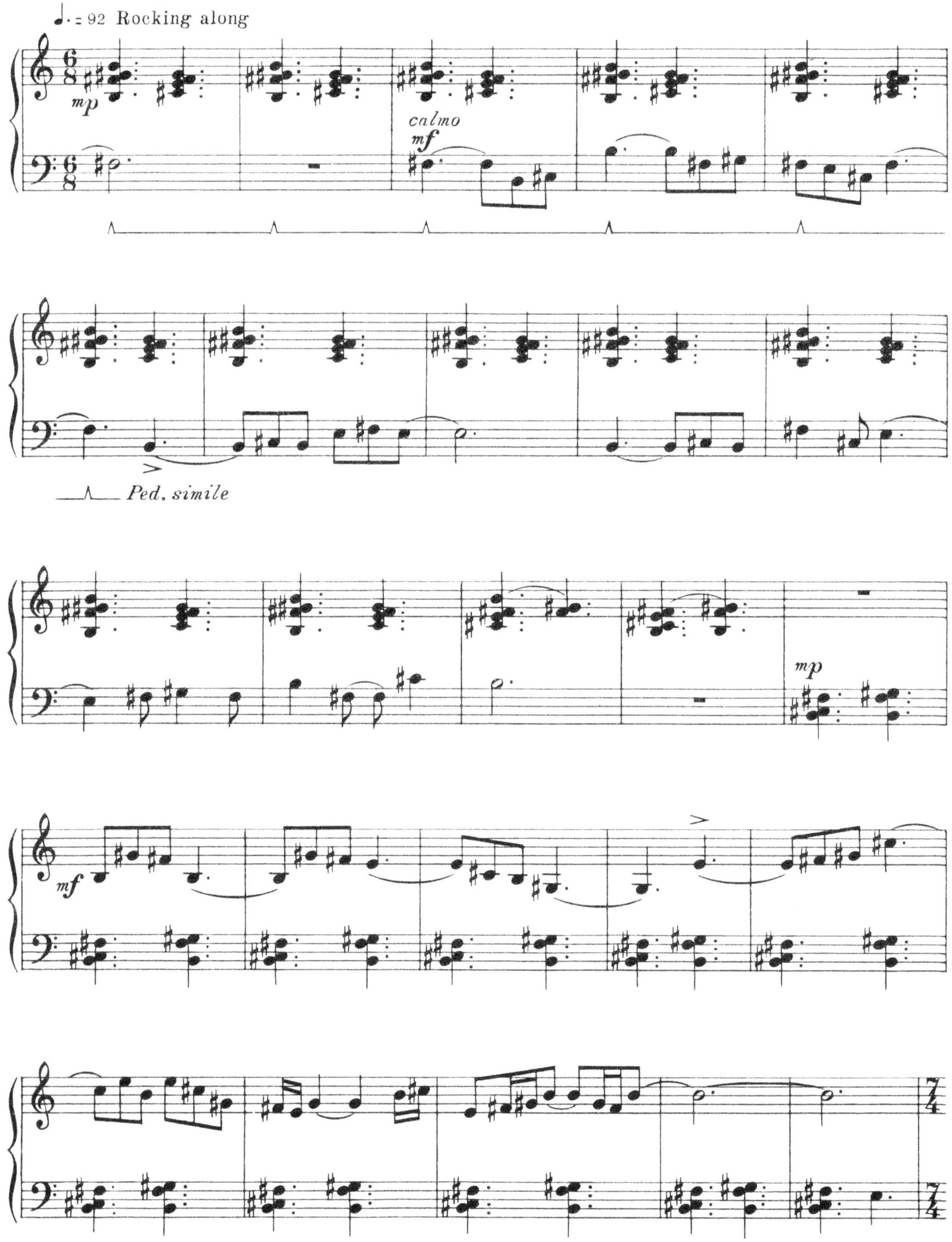

= 92 Rocking along
mp
calmo
mf
Ped. simile
mp
mf

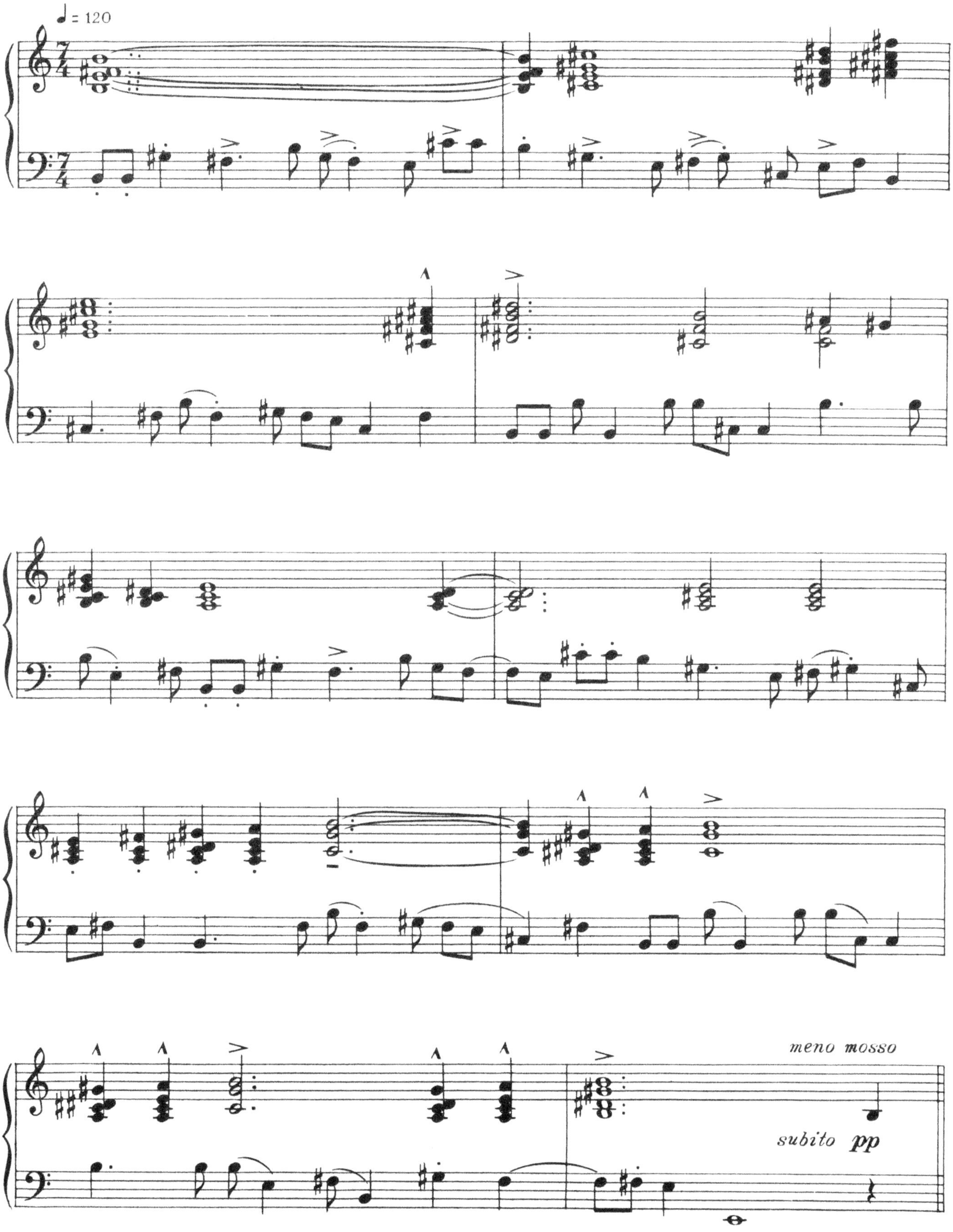
♩ = 120
meno mosso
subito pp

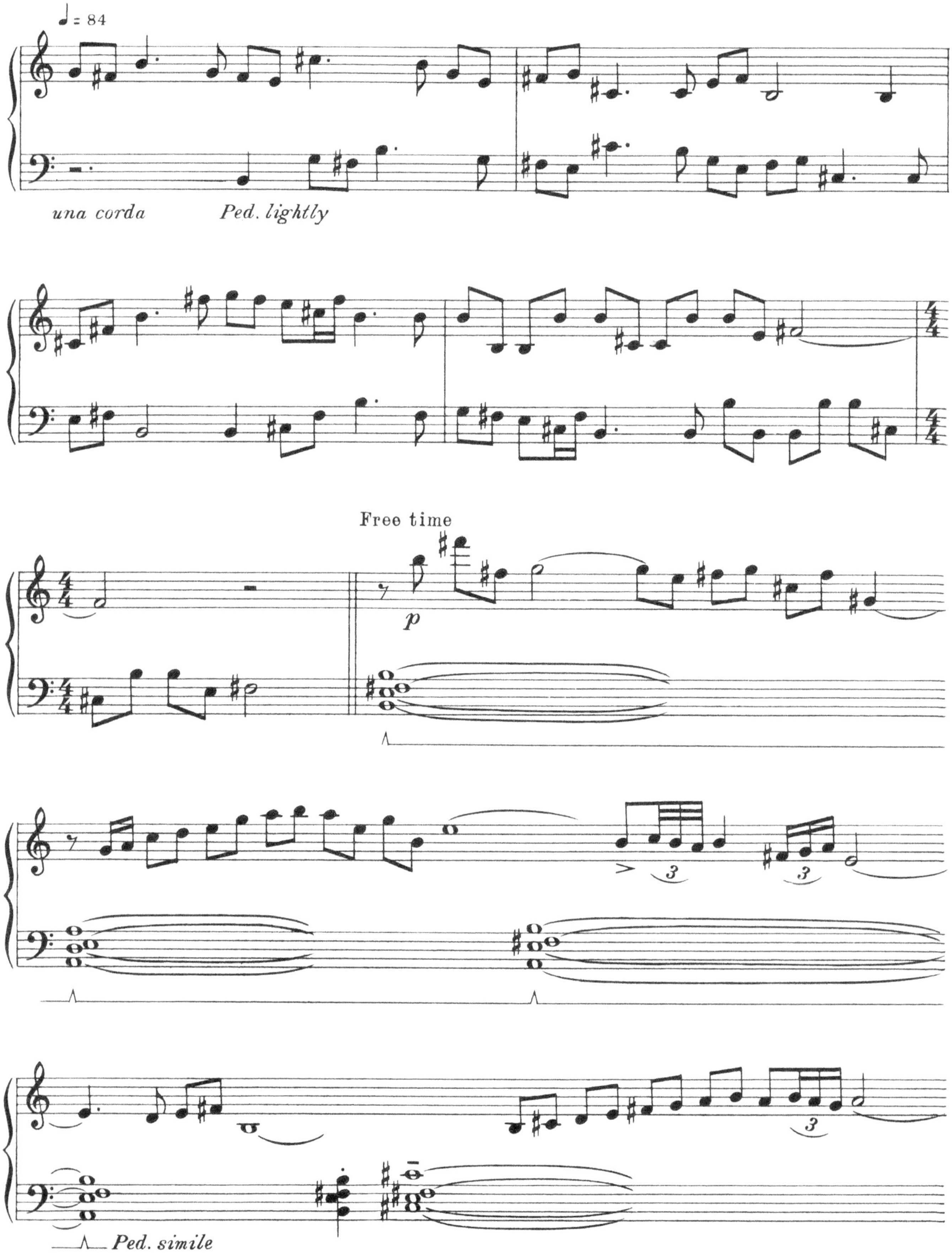
♩= 84
una corda
Ped. lightly
Free time
p
Ped. simile

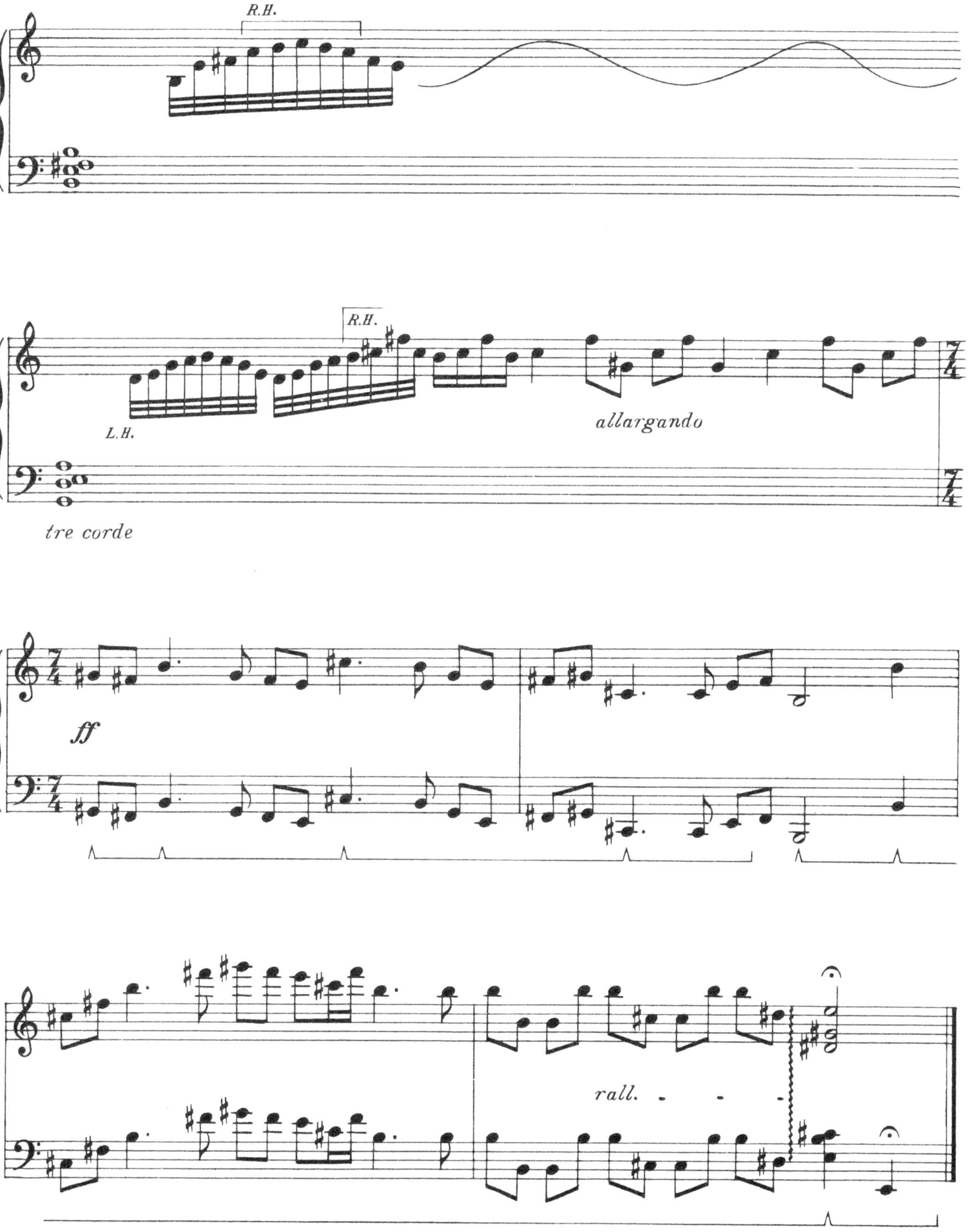
R.H.
L.H.
R.H.
allargando
tre corde
ff
rall.

Mini-Suite

Margaret S. Brandman

Allegretto ♩= 72

© Copyright 2020 Margaret Brandman Trading as Jazzem Music.
International copyright secured. APRA/AMCOS. All rights reserved.
Photocopying is illegal.

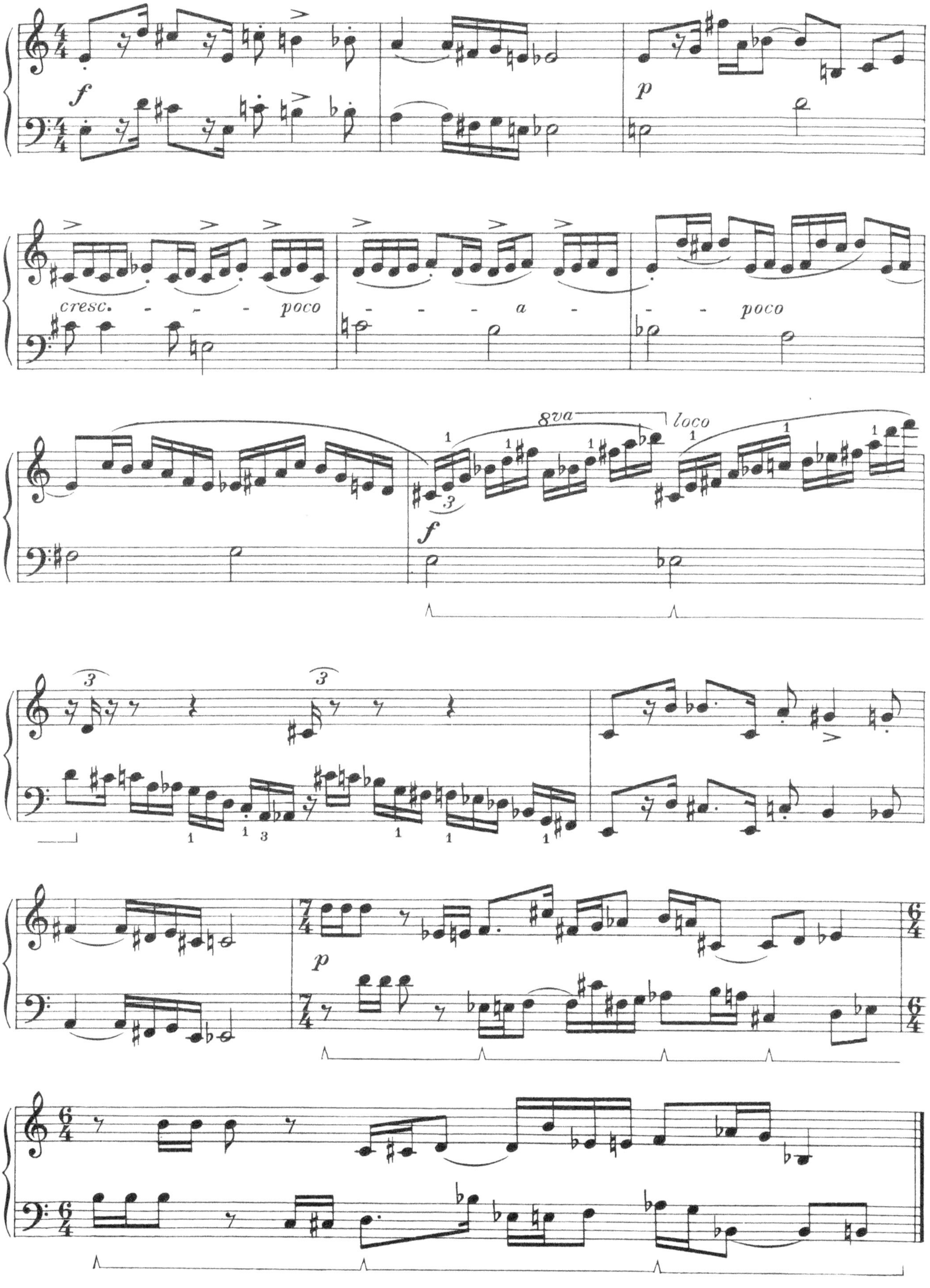
f
p
cresc. - - - poco
- - - - a -
- - poco
8va
loco
f
p

1x mp
2x mf
con Ped.
cresc.
1
2
f
mp
p
cresc.
rall.
Broadly
f
rall. e dim.
p

www.ingramcontent.com/pod-product-compliance
Lightning Source LLC
Chambersburg PA
CBHW080858090426
42737CB00015B/2989